FEEDING THE MIND

FEEDING THE MIND

BY

LEWIS CARROLL

WITH A PREFATORY NOTE BY

WILLIAM H. DRAPER

KALPAZ

ISBN: 978-93-5128-708-7(PB)

First Published in 1907
Indian Reprint in 2017

Published by

Kalpaz Publications
C-30, Satyawati Nagar,
Delhi – 110052
E-mail: kalpaz@hotmail.com
Website: kalpazpublications.com
Ph.: +91-9212142040

NOTE

THE *history of this little sparkle from the pen of Lewis Carroll may soon be told. It was in October of the year* 1884 *that he came on a visit to a certain vicarage in Derbyshire, where he had promised, on the score of friendship, to do what was for him a most unusual favour—to give a lecture before a public audience.*

The writer well remembers his nervous, highly-strung manner as he stood before the little room full of simple people, few of whom had any idea of the world-wide reputation of that shy, slight figure before them.

NOTE

When the lecture was over, he handed the manuscript to me, saying: 'Do what you like with it.'

The one for whose sake he did this kindness was not long after called

'Into the Silent Land.'

So the beautifully-written MS., in his customary violet ink, has been treasured for more than twenty years, only now and then being read over at Christmas-time to a friend or two by the study fire, always to meet with the same welcome and glad acknowledgment that here was a genuine, though little flame that could not have belonged to any other source but that which all the world knew in Alice in Wonderland *and* Through the Looking-Glass.

There may be, perhaps, many others who, gathering round a winter fire, will be glad to read words, however few, from that bright source, and whose memories will respond to the fresh touch of that cherished name.

It remains to add but one or two more associations that cling to it and make the remembrance more vivid still. While Lewis Carroll was staying in the house, there came to call a certain genial and by no means shy Dean, who, without realizing what he was doing, proceeded, in the presence of other callers, to make some remark identifying Mr. Dodgson as the author of his books.

There followed an immense explosion immediately on the visitor's departure, with a pathetic and serious request that, if there were any risk of a repetition of the call, due warning might be given, and the retreat secured.

NOTE

Probably not many readers of the immortal Alice have ever seen the curious little whimsical paper called

EIGHT OR NINE WISE WORDS

ABOUT

LETTER-WRITING

which their author had printed and used to send to his acquaintance, accompanied by a small case for postage-stamps.

It consists of forty pages, and is published by Emberlin and Son, Oxford; and these are the contents:

	PAGE
ON STAMP-CASES - - -	5
HOW TO BEGIN A LETTER -	8
HOW TO GO ON WITH A LETTER	11
HOW TO END A LETTER - -	20
ON REGISTERING CORRESPONDENCE	22

In this little script, also, there are the same sparkles of wit which betoken